D1102991

THE OFFICIAL

Care for Your

Pony

CONTENTS

HarperCollins*Publishers*

First published in 1981 by
William Collins Sons & Co Ltd, London
Revised edition 1985

New edition published in 1994
by HarperCollins Publishers
London

Reprinted 1994

This is a fully revised and extended edition of *Care for your Pony*, first
published in 1981 and reprinted with revisions in 1985

© Royal Society for the Prevention of Cruelty to Animals 1981, 1994

Text of the 1981 edition by Tina Hearne; text revisions and additions
for this edition by Angela Rixon

Designed and edited by The Templar Company plc
Pippbrook Mill, London Road, Dorking, Surrey RH4 1JE

Front cover photograph: Animal Ark, London
Text photographs: Angela Rixon

Illustrations by John Francis, George Friar and Sue Camm
Courtesy of Bernard Thornton Artists, London

**A catalogue record for this book is available
from the British Library**

ISBN 0 00 412732 3

Produced by HarperCollins Hong Kong

First things first, animals are fun. Anybody who has ever enjoyed the company of a pet knows well enough just how strong the bond between human and animal can be. Elderly or lonely people often depend on a pet for their only company, and this can be a rewarding relationship for both human and animal. Doctors have proved that animals can be instrumental in the prevention of and recovery from mental or physical disease. Children learn the meaning of loyalty, unselfishness and friendship by growing up with animals.

But the commitment to an animal doesn't begin and end with a visit to the local pet shop. A pet should never be given as a 'surprise' present. The decision to bring a pet into your home should always be discussed and agreed by all the members of your family. Bear in mind that parents are ultimately responsible for the health and well-being of the animal for the whole of its lifetime. If you are not prepared for the inevitable expense, time, patience and occasional frustration involved, then the RSPCA would much rather that you didn't have a pet.

Armed with the facts, aware of the pitfalls but still confident of your ability to give a pet a good home, the next step is to find where you can get an animal from. Seek the advice of a veterinary surgeon or RSPCA Inspector about reputable local breeders or suppliers. Do consider the possibility of offering a home to an animal from an RSPCA establishment. There are no animals more deserving of loving owners.

As for the care of your pet, you should find in this book all you need to know to keep it happy, healthy and rewarding for many years to come. Responsible ownership means happy pets. Enjoy the experience!

Terence C. Bate

TERENCE BATE BVSc, LLB, MRCVS
Chief Veterinary Officer, RSPCA

Introduction

Owning and caring for a pony can be one of the most rewarding experiences in life. It teaches self-discipline and self-reliance and helps to develop a sense of responsibility in young people. In return for good care, a pony will provide years of pleasure and a wonderful way to get and stay fit.

But ponies can be extremely demanding animals in terms of time, land and money. There may seem nothing to match the fervour of a child's longing for his or her own pony, but if parents do not give the matter careful thought, or if they make a hasty purchase, then they may find out too late that they have created an impossible situation.

A pony must have daily attention at regular times not just when its owner finds it convenient. It must have a safe, well-fenced field or paddock, and field shelter if it is to live out all year. The field must be well-drained and preferably large enough to divide into two or three sections to allow for controlled grazing. If the pony is to be stabled during the winter, a loose box of adequate size must be provided, with plenty of bedding, changed daily. The cost of winter feed is another factor to be considered before taking on ownership of a pony, for even hardy ponies which live out all year need supplementary food from late autumn to early summer. There will also be regular blacksmith's and vet's bills to be taken into account.

It may seem easy to a child to take on responsibility for his or her own pony, particularly if the child has learnt to ride at riding school, and perhaps enjoyed helping out there. But there is a world of difference between helping out occasionally, and having total control over the pony's daily routine. There is also a considerable difference between working (however hard) under knowledgeable guidance, and suddenly having to make all the decisions yourself.

If you decide it is impossible to buy your own pony, or to keep it at home, it is often feasible to arrange a half or quarter share with others, or to buy your pony and keep it at livery at a local stables. Many riding schools offer this facility and for the inexperienced owner this compromise ensures that the pony's welfare is monitored at all times.

Choosing a pony

Caring for a pony is great fun as well as a lot of hard work.

A good family pony may be of any shape or size, but it must be fit and active, healthy and hardy enough to live outside throughout the year. It need not be of any particular breed, but must be strong enough to carry all those members of the family who wish to ride, and be kind enough in temperament to respond to the aids of the youngest or smallest equestrians of the family. Most important of all, it must have a gentle, intelligent nature, be unafraid of traffic, and have no really bad habits.

Size and conformation   Though a small pony is ideal for a very small child who might feel unsafe on a larger animal, small ponies are often outgrown within a year or two, and in any case, are unsuitable for family use. A pony of 13 to 14 hands high is generally large enough to carry adults at slow paces, and small enough for a fairly young child to manage. Ponies in this size range also tend to have better temperament and manners than very small ponies.

The family pony does not necessarily have to be handsome, but should have a shape good enough to ensure a regular, steady movement. Straight shoulders produce a jerky action, and a very narrow chest may cause the front legs to brush together, making the pony unsafe to ride. A pony with a very short neck, or one with a narrow, upcurved 'ewe' neck will be equally uncomfortable to ride and will have an unnatural head carriage, causing it to canter and jump in an ungainly manner. The withers should be well developed to prevent the saddle sliding forwards, and a short, well-muscled back and strong hindquarters will ensure that the saddle does not slide backwards.

What age and sex?   Geldings are probably best for general riding, though mares are said to be more affectionate and intelligent. A gelding will perform steadily at all times while a mare can be a problem when she is in season. Young ponies are not suitable for novice riders, but are generally cheaper than experienced ponies. Very old ponies may not be capable of much strenuous work, but might prove ideal for a small or nervous child or adult. The best age for a family pony is between seven and twelve years, when it will be old enough to be steady and sensible, and young enough to provide several useful years in the same home. A pony of suitable height and conformation, carefully broken in but needing further schooling should be reasonably priced and in experienced hands could turn out to be the ideal all-round family pony. A pony may continue to grow until it is five or six years old and so these early years are important, being formative both mentally and physically.

HOW TO FIND THE RIGHT PONY

There are many ways to find a suitable family pony. Specialist magazines and papers carry pages of advertisements describing ponies for sale. It is best, however, to acquire a pony whose history and habits are well known, either from friends, or on the recommendation of a vet. A novice should always be accompanied by a knowledgeable friend when trying out a new pony, and the experienced rider should ride the pony at all paces as well as on the road. It is advisable to have a pony you are proposing to buy thoroughly examined by a vet before completing the purchase, and in some cases the seller will agree to a pony being taken home on trial for a week or so to ensure that it is wholly suitable.

When selecting a pony, ask to see it being caught up from the field, and watch it being groomed and tacked up. Some ponies are difficult to catch, some pretend to bite and kick while being groomed and saddled, while others bite and kick in earnest. It is sensible to pick up the pony's feet one by one; if it is unshod, it could mean that it is difficult or even impossible to shoe. Ponies turned out for the summer usually have their shoes removed, however, and it is possible to check the pony's temperament with its regular blacksmith.

Finding the right pony is only one aspect of choosing and buying a family or child's pony. A new owner must have a strong sense of commitment and be prepared to learn everything necessary to care for the animal correctly and consistently. More ponies suffer through ignorance, thought-lessness and selfishness than through deliberate cruelty.

During his examination the vet will check the pony's heart.

Dartmoor

Breeds

Children's riding ponies in Britain are nearly all descended from the nine native breeds that evolved in the mountains and moorlands of the British Isles. They are named accordingly: New Forest, Dartmoor, Exmoor, Welsh, Fell, Dales, Highland, Shetland and Connemara.

Ponies derived from these native breeds are particularly suitable for keeping at grass, being tough and hardy enough to tolerate harsh weather conditions, and so independent that they will even try to scratch a living in snow. If they are to be kept out all year they must never be clipped, nor even groomed excessively, because a long winter coat is their protection against the cold and rain.

But just because a pony is a hardy breed does not mean it can be left to fend for itself. Even if kept at grass all year, a field shelter should be provided (see pages 16–19) and all the usual care taken in feeding and grooming.

Connemara   This beautiful, even-tempered pony evolved in the windswept areas of western Ireland. Most commonly found in various shades of grey, there are also black, brown, bay and dun Connemaras, and until recently dun ponies with black dorsal stripes were common in the region. In the nineteenth century, Arabian stallions were run with the mares and the Arab influence is evident in the fine heads of the ponies. At 13–14 hands, the Connemara makes an ideal riding pony and an excellent jumper.

Dales   Larger and heavier than its close cousin the Fell, the Dales pony can be up to 14.2 hands high and is usually black, bay or dark brown. It is exceptionally strong with a true pony head, short strong neck, straight shoulders and a muscular back. The heels are feathered. Ponies of this breed are extensively used for driving and in agriculture but make ideal riding ponies, able to carry the heaviest of adults.

Dartmoor   This is an extremely pretty breed, standing no more than 12.2 hands. It makes a very good riding pony if handled young. Known for its hardiness, the Dartmoor is able to withstand, in the wild state, the harsh weather conditions on the moors, which are notorious for their windswept bleakness in winter.

Dales

Connemara

Exmoor Most ancient of the British breeds and said to be a direct descendant of the native British wild horse, the Exmoor pony is distinguished by its rich brown colouring and the pale oaten or 'mealy' markings around its eyes and on its muzzle. At 12.2 hands high the Exmoor is ideal for small children to ride, being narrow and sure-footed. It is also capable of carrying an adult across rough terrain, and makes an ideal driving pony.

Fell The Fell pony is a heavy breed used originally for draught and pack work, but now makes a useful family pony, gentle enough to be ridden by a small child and strong enough to carry a heavy man. It is generally black, though brown is sometimes seen and the occasional bay, and has an abundant waved mane and tail and feathered heels. Up to 14 hands high, the Fell is lively and alert with a smooth fast trot which it can maintain for miles, and is very hardy.

Highland Perhaps the most versatile of the British native ponies, the Highland has become more popular in recent years. Varying in height between 13 and 14.2 hands, they have been used as pack ponies for generations, but are now regarded as the ideal family pony – strong enough to carry adults and gentle enough to be trusted with small children. Perhaps the most interesting feature of the Highland is the great range of colours in which it may be found. In addition to grey, black and brown there are bays, liver-chestnuts with silver manes and tails, and many variations of dun from the silver mouse-dun through cream, silver and gold.

New Forest   An attractive and reliable riding pony, the New Forest makes a very safe ride for children. It has a reputation for being good in traffic, as it is so used to the people and vehicles in the Forest. It can be any solid colour (that is, not piebald or skewbald) and is one of our larger pony breeds, standing between 12 and 14 hands.

Shetland   Well-known and popular, this little pony, standing less than 10.2 hands, is often first choice as a young child's first mount, although not always with complete success since its stout body makes it rather wide between the child's knees. For its size, this is probably the strongest pony in the world, able to survive the severest weather conditions and rough grazing.

Welsh Cob (C)

Welsh Mountain (A)

Welsh   This pretty breed is divided into four types, referred to as Sections A, B, C and D. The smallest of the four is the **Welsh Mountain Pony** (Section A), and is obviously the breed from which the other types have sprung. The Welsh Mountain is up to 12 hands high and of any solid colour.

The **Welsh Pony** (Section B) is a little larger, being up to 12.2 hands high and makes a top-class riding and show pony.

Welsh Cobs (Sections C and D) are similar in general conformation, being sturdily built and with a pronounced free-trotting action. Section C may measure up to 13.2 hands high while the Section D Cob, although a pony in its characteristics, may be as tall as 15.2.

Biology

Ungulates The horse, *Equus caballus*, is an ungulate, a word derived from *unguis*, the Latin name for a hoof. The hoofed beasts subdivide into the even-toed group, which includes swine, bovines and deer; and the odd-toed beasts, of which the horses – zebras, asses and true horses – form the largest family.

The earliest horse, the so-called Dawn horse, Eohippus, grazed on swampland vegetation in North American about 70 million years ago. It is known to have had four toes on each forefoot and three on each hindfoot. The gradual evolution of the foot is considered an adaptation to a changing environment.

Modern horses walk on just the tip of the third toe, which has become centralized, and dominant, and greatly strengthened by a surrounding hoof. This highly specialized foot is particularly adapted to moving at speed on hard ground such as steppe-lands and prairies.

In the wild state these fleet, long-legged grassland animals rely on speed to escape such natural predators as the large carnivores – for instance, the leopard. They have also developed the social structure of the herd which, with the remarkably wide range of vision of the horse, gives good advance warning of danger.

Horse or pony? There is no exact definition of the word 'pony'. Perhaps it should be said at once that a pony is not a young horse, and never grows into a horse. The pony breeds are recognized as quite distinct from the horse breeds, although both are *Equus caballus*.

The principal difference is in the size of the mature animal, and most authorities agree that breeds standing less than 14.2 hands/ approx. 145 cm are ponies. Even so, there are exceptions to such rules. For instance, a little Arab mare, standing only 13.2 hands, is a horse, together with all other Arabs; while a polo pony of almost 16 hands is still a pony.

In general, and despite all the variations that occur, the pony breeds are small, hardy animals, with a compact body and powerful quarters standing on short, sturdy legs. It can be seen from the native British breeds that they also have great qualities of endurance, strength and resourcefulness. Their reasonable size and intelligence make them ideal breeds for children.

Size The height is measured at the withers, preferably using a measuring stick. In the United Kingdom, horses and ponies are measured in 'hands' and inches. One hand is 4 in/ approx. 10 cm. Thus a height of 12.1 denotes 12 hands and 1 inch (approx. 125 cm); 12.2 is 12 hands and 2 inches, and so on.

Herbivores The horse is an excellent example of an animal specially adapted to live by grazing grass, without needing to chew the cud as do the ruminant animals. All the herbivores have a very long gut, for the better assimilation of a high fibre diet. To some extent the extensive development of the large intestine in the horse compensates for the lack of the complex ruminant stomach.

The horse's stomach is relatively small, and therefore restricts the amount of feed that can be taken at one time. For this reason it is necessary for ponies to feed regularly and frequently, on fairly small amounts, and they will take feed not only during the day, but also during the night.

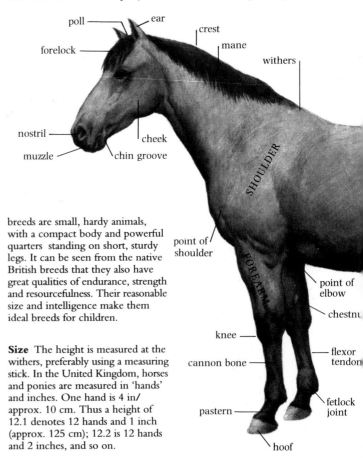

poll — ear

forelock —

crest

mane

withers

nostril —

cheek

muzzle — chin groove

SHOULDER

point of shoulder

FOREARM

point of elbow

chestnu

knee —

cannon bone —

flexor tendon

pastern —

fetlock joint

hoof

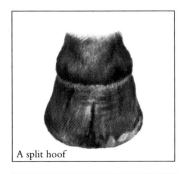

A split hoof

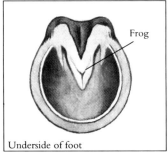

Frog

Underside of foot

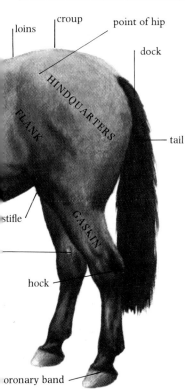

loins
croup
point of hip
dock
HINDQUARTERS
FLANK
tail
stifle
GASKIN
hock
coronary band

Feet One of the best-known of the old sayings about horses asserts 'No foot – no horse', and the proper care of the pony's feet is of the greatest importance. It is easier to understand this if you have a basic knowledge of the structure of the foot.

The weight is taken partly on the wall of the foot, which is the hard, horny hoof, and partly on the frog, which is made of a softer, more rubbery horn which acts as a shock-absorber, giving springiness to the gait and helping to prevent slipping. Between the wall and the frog is the concave sole, which is made of soft horn that flakes away.

The wall of the hoof lies on a sensitive quick. When the under surface of a cleaned and prepared foot is examined a 'white line' can be seen, which marks this division between the sensitive and insensitive parts of the foot.

The hoof grows downwards from the coronary band, although more at the toe than the heel. In the wild state the hoof wears down naturally on hard ground. Domesticated ponies kept unshod at grass may be on too soft a surface for their hooves to wear away. If a pony's hooves are allowed to grow too long they may split, break, or grow out of shape.

If a pony is kept shod for riding, the hoof will not be worn away by friction. This means that regular removal of shoes and trimming of the hoof is necessary to maintain correct shape of the foot, correct contact of the frog with the ground and a proper positioning of the shoe on the foot.

All ponies need to be seen regularly by a farrier, about every six weeks, and immediately if there is any trouble between visits, such as a cast shoe or risen clenches (shoe-nails) in the wall of the foot. A good farrier will be able to give invaluable advice about keeping your pony's feet in good order.

Note If a shoe sounds as if it has become loose while you are out riding, dismount and lead your pony home. Similarly, if you notice that the pony has gone lame, dismount immediately and investigate. The trouble may be no more than a stone, which you will be able to remove yourself. In the case of more serious lameness, lead the pony home slowly and call a veterinary surgeon.

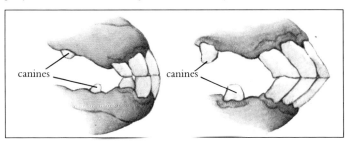

canines

canines

Teeth The horse's dentition is well adapted to tearing grass with the incisors, and grinding it between the molars before swallowing. In many ponies these molar teeth wear to produce sharp and ragged edges which require occasional rasping. If this is neglected there may be difficulty with feeding and subsequent loss of condition, and soreness of the cheeks. The angle of the incisor teeth gives a clue to the age of the horse. The illustration on the left shows those of a four-year-old, while that on the right shows the incisors of a 13-year-old, by which age the angle has become much more acute.

The canines (the tushes) are not needed for feeding by a complete herbivore, such as the horse. Stallions will sometimes use them as weapons but they are either absent or merely rudimentary in the mare.

The stabled pony

There are two basic methods of keeping a pony. Either it iş 'in', which means it is stabled, ideally within easy reach of a paddock or field where it may be turned out occasionally; or it is 'out', which means it is kept at grass, with a field shelter for occasional use.

Of the two systems, living in requires a far higher degree of competence in general management of the pony, and is the less common. It may not be advisable to keep your own pony in permanently, unless it has to work.

Ponies are, by nature, wide-ranging herd animals with remarkable qualities of independence and self-sufficiency, and almost certainly would prefer to live out. Nevertheless, in practice it is desirable to have a stable available, even if the intention is to keep the pony out at grass whenever possible.

There are many times when it is necessary, or more convenient, or more comfortable for the pony to be kept in: when it is ill or injured; when the weather is very cold or wet; when there is deep snow; when the flies are particularly troublesome in summer; when the grass is growing so fast in spring that it is necessary to restrict feeding; and when diet and exercise need to be planned to improve the pony's condition ready for competition, or any increase in work.

A basic stable routine should be established along the following lines:

A waterproof New Zealand rug protects a pony kept outside in cold wet weather.

early morning	check pony; check supply of fresh water; tie up with small hay feed while stable is mucked out; pick out feet	first feed
after exercise	check supply of fresh water; groom and put on day rug	second feed or grazing
late afternoon	remove droppings; pick out feet; shake up bedding and add more if necessary; check water; put on night rug	third feed
evening	remove droppings; check water	hay and fourth feed

Mucking out Early every morning the pony must be tied up with hay and fresh water while the stable is mucked out. The droppings and soiled bedding are removed to a manure heap, and the dry bedding forked to the sides of the box. Sweep or wash the floor and leave it to dry.

Bedding It is not good for ponies to stand on concrete or stable-brick floors for long periods, so those confined to the stable, for whatever reason, may need a day bed later in the morning. This is made by spreading the remaining straw back over the floor, once it has dried. Bedding is best made of wheat straw, but alternatives include peat litter or sawdust and shavings.

The night bed, made up in late afternoon, is deep and banked up around the sides and door. Ponies sleep fitfully, often standing, but a good bed encourages them to lie down and benefit from more complete rest.

Grooming Every day a stabled horse must be well groomed for 45–60 minutes. Ponies must also have their feet picked out every day before and after work.

Clothing To keep the clipped pony warm during cold weather, it is covered with a rug and, often, a woollen blanket beneath for extra warmth at night. In hot weather, the pony may need a fly-sheet to protect it from insects when it is turned out in a paddock.

Exercise Ponies should be exercised every day. They tend to become bored with being stabled, and on their weekly rest day it is important to turn them out – in a waterproof New Zealand rug if need be – to roam free in a paddock or field.

Food Three or four feeds, evenly spaced throughout the day, are needed, with additional hay for the night. A manger fixed at a convenient height or feed bowls standing on the floor are both acceptable.

Water Ponies drink more when stabled than when out at grass: several gallons (1 gal = 4.5 l) a day. Check that clean water is available throughout the day and night. Periodically scrub out the water containers.

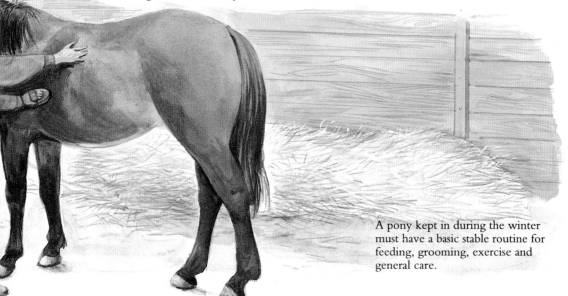

A pony kept in during the winter must have a basic stable routine for feeding, grooming, exercise and general care.

The loose box

The site It is most important that the stabling is sited on hard standing, and serviced with running water, drainage and electricity. The best aspect is south-facing, and a roof overhang will give protection from the rain both to the ponies looking out of their boxes and to the handler in rainy weather.

Stable buildings There is a wide range of manufactured stabling available, usually made of timber, and varying from a single loose box to a range of boxes with a tack room. Brick remains the best construction material available for more permanent stabling. Each pony will need its own box. An adequate size for a pony's box would be 3 x 3 m/10 x 10 ft, allowing room for the pony to turn round and lie down in comfort. A larger box would be even better and much easier to work in, although too large a box is wasteful of bedding.

Stable doors These open outwards, to prevent the bedding being disturbed every time the door is used, and to allow the best possible access should a pony become 'cast' in the box, that is, unable to get up off the floor.

The door must be wide enough for the pony to pass through easily, without bruising itself or damaging the saddlery.

The divided door allows plenty of light and fresh air into the box, and gives the pony the chance to look out and take an interest in the stable yard, while remaining safely contained.

Flooring Ponies can slip on smooth or wet flooring. The best flooring is made of special 'stable-bricks', but roughened concrete is an acceptable alternative. There should always be enough bedding to prevent slipping at all times.

Secure bolts At least two secure bolts must be used on the lower half of the stable door because some ponies become adept at opening doors. The top half merely requires a suitable latch which will not harm the pony's eye. There should also be some method of securing the top half of the door open.

Ventilation It is very important for the pony's health for it to be kept in a well-ventilated stable. The ventilation must never be drastically reduced in an attempt to keep the pony warm. Instead, add another blanket beneath its rug.

Draughts Ponies are susceptible to draughts, and the stable should be as free of them as possible. A louvred ventilator sited high in the gable end of the stable keeps the loose box well ventilated, yet the pony clear of draughts.

Windows In addition to providing light, windows can provide additional ventilation in hot weather. Bars or netting may be necessary on the inside to prevent a pony putting its head through the glass, and to avoid accidents with the handle of a tool when mucking out.

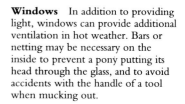

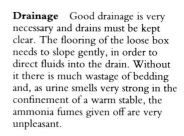

Drainage Good drainage is very necessary and drains must be kept clear. The flooring of the loose box needs to slope gently, in order to direct fluids into the drain. Without it there is much wastage of bedding and, as urine smells very strong in the confinement of a warm stable, the ammonia fumes given off are very unpleasant.

Fittings A good loose box has the minimum of fittings, so that neither the pony nor the saddlery becomes entangled. Light switches are best placed outside the loose box. The only fittings needed inside are a tie ring for the pony and a bracket to hold the water bucket; a manger and perhaps an automatic drinking bowl can also be fitted. It is very dangerous to have nails sticking out of the stable wall.

Forage room The forage room should be near or next to the loose boxes. Feedstuff stored here should be kept in vermin-proof bins.

Tack room Tack should preferably be kept in a tack room – certainly not left lying around. It is all expensive and vulnerable to damage, and, if it is not kept in good condition, may become uncomfortable or dangerous to use. Tack is often stolen, but may be branded under the flaps with the owner's name. The tack room, which may be combined with the forage room, should be kept securely locked to deter casual theft.

The pony at grass

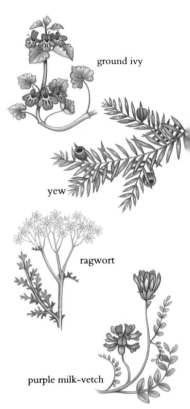

ground ivy

yew

ragwort

purple milk-vetch

Keeping a pony at grass, with a field shelter, is the easiest system of management for the owner, but, even so, it may take a considerable time each day.

Ponies descended from hardy native breeds are quite able to live at grass throughout the year. They will, however, certainly need a field shelter to compensate for the lack of natural protection which will not be available in a field or paddock.

Although a pony at grass is more self-sufficient than a stable-bound one, you will still need to visit at least once a day to ensure all is well and to forge close bonds with your pony. It should be examined all over for any cuts or injury, and its feet cleaned and rug checked. At the same time the water supply should be checked and droppings and litter cleared. Take your pony a treat and spend time getting to know each other.

The pasture   Each pony needs 0.5 or 1 hectare/1 or 2 acres of pasture, preferably divided in two, so that the parts of the field may be used in rotation. Grass needs managing like any other crop, and should be chain harrowed, limed or fertilized each year as necessary. Do not turn ponies on to the grass until the fertilizer has been well washed in, and if weed-killers are used, they must be kept off the land for at least two weeks. Land drains need to be kept in good repair and ditches clear.

Ponies living on small areas that are intensively grazed are constantly being reinfected with intestinal worm larvae which are eliminated with the dung, and then reingested with the grass. This is why it is important to pick up the droppings every day. Each pony at grass needs to be wormed at least twice a year.

Boundaries   The field must be bounded by a good stock-proof hedge or post and rail fencing. Palings, whether made of iron or wood, are potentially dangerous, as is wire, whether plain or barbed. The gate must have a secure catch that the pony cannot learn to open. The gate catch should be positioned so that it can be reached from a riding position.

It is important to have strong, secure fences which will stand firm even when subjected to a pony's substantial weight.

It is not safe to assume that the pony will avoid poisonous plants. In particular the hedgerow and banks should be kept clear of such plants as ground ivy, black bryony and nightshades. Remember that many ornamental trees and shrubs such as yew and laburnum can be very poisonous. If you are unsure about any plants in your field, ask someone who can identify poisonous varieties.

black bryony

deadly nightshade

laburnum

Being naturally gregarious, ponies are more contented when they live and graze together.

Water supply   Because water is so heavy to carry, it really is better if the field has its own piped water supply. If the land is divided into two or more sections, for use in rotation, then each section will need its own water trough, or tank, large enough to hold two or three days' supply.

Dangerous litter   When checking the field, it is important to pick up any dangerous litter. Items such as broken glass, rusty pieces of iron and discarded tin cans may cause the pony injury. They can gradually work their way up to the surface even if they were once buried.

Clothing   In the winter a grass-kept pony may need a well-fitting New Zealand rug. This is a waterproof rug with a wool lining, which is secured by straps around the hind legs (see page 12). You should check every day that the rug has not shifted position.

Companionship   It is not a good idea to have too many ponies in one field because of the risks of overgrazing, cutting up of the grass and fighting. Nevertheless a pony is a social animal and may be very unhappy if kept alone: donkeys or goats make very suitable companions if there is no other pony to share the field.

The paddock

This is the arrangement to aim at if you are thinking of keeping a pony at home, although such an ideal arrangement is only practical where there is plenty of land available near the house.

In this case the pony has the companionship of a donkey, and because both the paddock and stable are adjacent to the house and garden, there will be plenty of human contact.

Having a paddock within sight of the house, as well as being a joy for the owners, is the best possible safety precaution. There is far less risk of interference to the pony, the fencing or the gates by passers-by, than is possible when the pony is kept elsewhere. In particular, there is less likelihood of the pony being fed unsuitable or even dangerous titbits.

When this close, the pony can be seen easily, and moved into the field shelter when necessary. All the attention needed is so much more easily and willingly done with the pony so close at hand.

broken glass

barbed wire

ragwort

A field shelter must always be provided, although it is often refused by the hardiest ponies. It will give them protection on cold and blustery nights, and also a refuge from flies in summer. The shelter should be built facing south on well-drained land, preferably on hard standing, and needs a wide entrance and a weatherproof roof. It must be large enough to hold all the ponies kept in the field. There should be some method of confining the pony or ponies to the shelter when the farrier is visiting or when grazing needs to be restricted.

Keep the paddock clear of litter and ensure an inquisitive pony cannot reach harmful plants or injure itself on dangerous wire or nails.

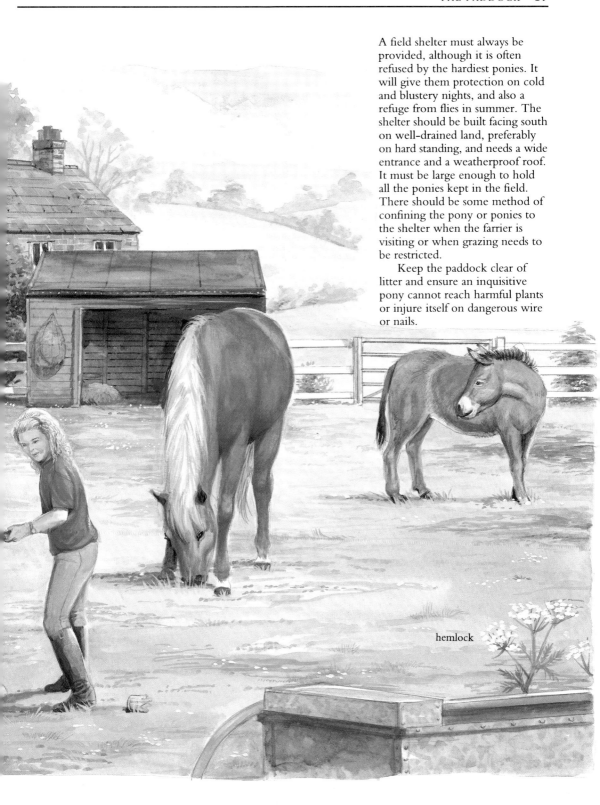

hemlock

Feeding and watering

A pony has a very small stomach in relation to its overall size, and the food that it eats takes up to 48 hours to pass through its complex digestive system.

The system depends on the pony taking in the correct amounts of food at the right time of the day, an adequate supply of fresh water and plenty of exercise. Wild ponies generally drink at dawn and dusk and in between follow a pattern of grazing, resting and exercise. To keep a pony healthy, this natural pattern is followed as closely as possible, feeding little and often, with plenty of bulk – grass or hay – and paying attention to the pony's work pattern.

A pony's staple diet is grass, or hay if it is stabled, and ponies in regular hard work need additional food to keep them fit and well-muscled.

Several manufacturers produce excellent ready-mixed feeds for ponies, graded for the animals' workload, and with detailed feeding tables on the packaging. Feed merchants have leaflets available on request.

FEEDING

The stabled pony The stabled pony will require a regular supply of hay – perhaps three hay racks a day – plus an appropriate quantity of 'short' feed, e.g. concentrates, bran or chaff. Again, supplementary feeding will depend on the workload. The traditional grain fed to working horses is crushed oats, but these can generally be fed only in moderation to children's riding ponies, since they may overstimulate the animal. Pony cubes may be more suitable.

Stabled ponies in particular seem to enjoy up to 1 kg/ 2 lb cut apples, or carrots sliced lengthwise.

The pony at grass Generally, the pony kept at grass must be allowed to graze as and when it wishes. The main exception to this rule is in the early spring, when the grass is particularly lush, and an excess of it can cause a variety of problems, including indigestion and laminitis (see Ailments, pages 36-37).

Hay should also be fed from a haynet or hay rack.

In the winter months, the grass grows very little and is low in nutritional content. At this time of year all ponies kept out will be dependent on hay, and may be expected to eat 1 tonne/1 ton during the winter.

If the grass-fed pony is expected to do any serious work, supplementary feeding will probably be needed, even during the summer, but never work a pony within one hour of feeding.

Grass is the perfect natural food for a pony, requiring supplementation only when the animal is required to do hard work, or in winter time.

Typical daily feeding requirements

	first feed	second feed	third feed	fourth feed
large pony out at night or part of the day	500 g/1 lb oats 500 g/1 lb bran 1 kg/2 lb cubes 1 kg/2 lb hay	500 g/1 lb oats 500 g/1 lb bran 1 kg/2 lb cubes 500 g/1 lb flaked maize 1.5 kg/3 lb hay	1 kg/2 lb oats 500 g/1 lb bran 500 g/1 lb cubes 500 g/1 lb carrots 3 kg/6 lb hay	
pony out briefly during day	500 g/1 lb bran 1 kg/2 lb cubes 1 kg/2 lb hay		1 kg/2 lb oats 500 g/1 lb bran	1 kg/2 lb oats 500 g/1 lb bran 500 g/1 lb cubes 3 kg/6 lb hay
small pony out for part of day and all night	500 g/1 lb bran 500 g/1 lb cubes 500 g/1 lb hay	500 g/1 lb bran 1 kg/2 lb cubes 1 kg/2 lb hay	500 g/1 lb oats 1 kg/2 lb bran 500 g/1 lb carrots 2.5 kg/5 lb hay	

FEEDSTUFFS

Hay   Good hay is gold and pale green in colour and smells sweet. Bad hay has dark brown parts in the bale, contains weeds and may smell musty. **Chaff** is chopped hay which adds bulk to the diet and prevents a greedy pony from eating too fast.

A pony's feed will need to be stored in large vermin-proof bins.

Pony cubes or **'nuts'**   These are manufactured in various mixes to provide a completely balanced diet for the pony. They contain plenty of roughage plus vitamins and minerals to keep the pony healthy.

Crushed oats   A concentrated high-energy food for working ponies; too many oats can make a pony difficult to control.

Barley   Another high-energy food and ideal for building up thin ponies or those recovering from illness. Whole barley must be boiled, then mixed with chaff or bran, though rolled barley can be fed on its own if necessary.

Flaked maize   This can be fed mixed with chaff or bran. It is rich, so very little is needed.

Bran   A good bulk food which can be fed dry with other hard food, dampened down slightly, or steeped in hot water to make a bran 'mash' which is ideal for giving to ponies which have had a very hard day's work at a show or rally.

GOOD TREATS

Washed carrots
(cut lengthwise)

Apple quarters

Pony cubes

BAD TREATS

Sweets
(peppermints, toffees etc.)

Sugar cubes

Fresh bread

Even a grass-fed pony will enjoy suitable treats such as carrots, apples and pony cubes.

WATERING

After exercise   There are many old tales about when to water a pony, and when not to. The modern view is that when a pony comes back thirsty, after exercise, it should be allowed about half a bucket immediately and more later when it has cooled off. In cold weather, water given to a hot pony should have the chill taken off by adding some hot water to the bucket.

When feeding   Clean water should always be available but it is advisable to encourage your pony to drink before being fed. If a lot of water is taken immediately after feeding, the effect is to wash undigested food from the stomach.

A clean, flowing stream will provide a refreshing drink.

Welsh Mountain pony

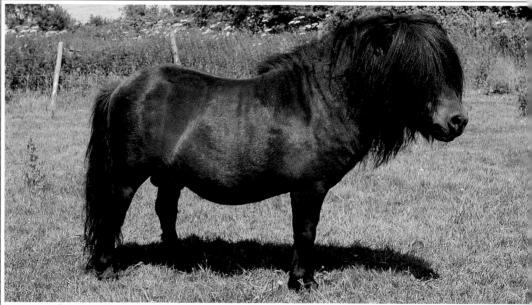

Miniature Shetland stallion

ighland pony running free

onnemara

Skewbald is a colouring, not a breed

Grooming

Ponies kept at grass are groomed very little, so that their natural oils can waterproof them against the weather, but stabled ponies need to be groomed every day. Stabled ponies may be clipped in the winter. Clipping is necessary because the long winter coat, which protects ponies from the weather, becomes a disadvantage when working, causing them to sweat excessively, to lose condition, and to dry off so slowly that they become chilled. If your pony is clipped, it should wear a rug. In very cold weather or at night it may also be necessary to put on a blanket underneath the rug.

Grooming is not just a matter of improving the appearance of the pony. It also cleans and massages the skin, and helps to maintain the pony's condition. Those who have their own pony will also know that it is one of the best ways of building up a pony's confidence and of enjoying its company for perhaps an hour a day.

Dandy brush   The dandy brush has stiff bristles and must be used with care, particularly on animals which are clipped or sensitive. Its particular purpose is to remove dried mud and loose hair from the coat. It should not be used on the mane or tail as it tends to split and break the hair.

Body brush   The body brush can be used on the whole body, the mane, tail and face. Its softer bristles are suitable for tender areas. It is the main implement for the removal of dirt, grease and dandruff from the coat.

Curry comb   The curry comb is used in conjunction with a body brush. After every few strokes, the body brush is drawn across the comb to be cleaned. The curry comb itself is never used on the pony.

Water brush   The water brush has soft bristles and is used damp to 'lay' the mane, or occasionally to assist in the final preparation of a mane or tail, for instance, prior to plaiting for show purposes.

Grooming tools of good quality an investment. Keep them clean and do not leave them lying arou

Mane comb

Water brush

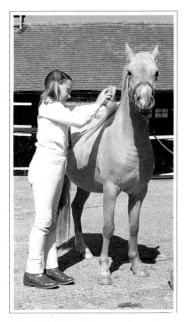

The dandy brush is used gently to remove mud and loose hairs.

Mane comb   This is a small metal comb which can be used to finish off the grooming of the mane after all the tangles have been removed.

Sponges   A damp sponge is used gently to clean the eyes, nostrils, mouth and dock. You ought to have two – one for use on the face and one on the dock.

Stable rubber   Stable rubbers are folded cloths, which may be used slightly damp to put a final shine on the pony's coat after grooming.

Hoof pick   Use the hoof pick every day to remove mud and small stones from the sole of the foot and the clefts either side of the frog. The hoof pick chosen must not have a very sharp point and should be drawn carefully from the heel down one cleft of the frog towards the toe, then down the other cleft in the same direction. Any remaining mud or stones are then picked out from inside the rim of the shoe. Always pick out your pony's hooves before and after exercise.

Hoof oil   Hoof oil is painted on to clean, well-dried hooves to prevent brittleness. It adds the final touch to a well-groomed pony.

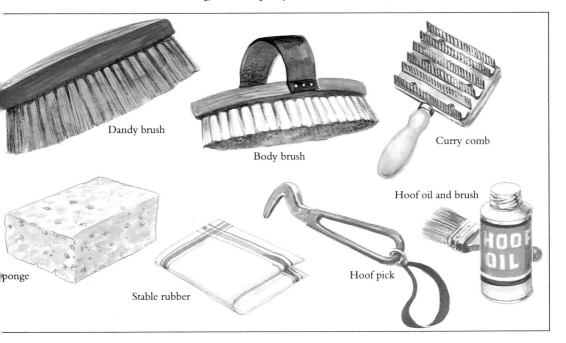

Dandy brush

Body brush

Curry comb

Hoof oil and brush

ponge

Stable rubber

Hoof pick

HOOF OIL

Handling

Ponies are extremely sensitive creatures and very easily upset. For this reason your general approach to them must be smooth, unhurried and consistent.

It is important to remember to approach a pony from the head and to speak as you do so. An unexpected approach will startle the pony and may make it awkward to handle.

When working with ponies be aware of your personal safety, and do not become careless, or take unreasonable liberties. Loose clothing, sudden noises, the slamming of doors, clattering buckets and any unexpected movement can very easily upset a pony, and again make it difficult to handle.

Catching a pony   To catch a pony in its field, approach with a headcollar – perhaps even hidden behind the back – so that the pony does not sense that it is to be caught. Many will come quickly if they are offered a few pony cubes or a carrot as a bribe. In general, it is probably better practice to offer the titbit as a reward when the pony has been caught.

When you reach the pony, gently put the shank around the neck to restrain the animal, while fitting the headcollar. If it is put on carelessly it may become head shy or difficult to catch.

It is very important not to chase the pony around its field. That might well become its favourite game, and your authority over it will be lost.

Hoof inspection   Most ponies are quite willing to lift their feet for inspection, because they are used to farriery and regular grooming. In most cases it is easy enough to observe the condition of the feet and the state of wear of the shoes.

Lift the forefeet by standing at the side of the pony facing the tail. Run your hand down the limb from the knee, circle the fetlock with the hand nearest the pony, lean your shoulder against the pony's leg, and lift the foot.

To lift a hind leg, move along the pony to the rear, talking calmly and running your hand along the back. Facing the tail, take your hand gently down the hind leg to the hoof, lean against the pony and lift.

The hoof pick is used to remove mud and stones gently from the underside of the pony's hooves.

Ponies are generally led on their handler's right hand side, and should move freely alongside on a slightly slack rein. This palomino is being led on a show bridle.

Never attempt to lift a foot when standing behind, or in front of the pony, and after checking the hoof, replace it gently on the ground and praise the pony.

Make sure that you always handle the limbs in a sensible manner.

Leading the pony   To lead a pony, walk on the left side at the pony's shoulder, holding the headcollar rope about 50 cm/18 in from the head in your right hand. Hold the long end of the rope in your left hand. It is dangerous to wind the rope around the hands because you could be pulled over if the pony suddenly shied or bolted.

When going through the stable door, walk ahead of the pony and lead it through carefully, taking care that it does not knock itself on the door posts.

If at any time the pony refuses to be led, be calm, try circling, and leading straight off. On no account must you start a tug-of-war. The pony will soon discover its superior strength, and not only resist you but also perhaps get into the very bad habit of pulling back. This can be hard to cure, and make a pony difficult for anyone to handle.

Horseboxes

If you hope eventually to take part in competitive events such as shows and gymkhanas, some form of transport will be necessary for your pony. It cannot be expected to hack to and from the showground in addition to competing. Several designs of horsebox and trailer are available, to cover differing budget and transport requirements.

Ponies need to be trained in order to go in and out of the horsebox in a safe, calm manner. The simplest way to load a pony is to lead it straight forward and up the ramp, resisting any temptation to pull at its head. A helper may stand behind in case any help is required but should be out of kicking range. The main reason for a pony's reluctance to enter a horsebox is the clatter of its hooves on the ramp. This can be largely overcome by laying straw on the ramp, and the pony may be encouraged by having a helper go ahead of the pony with a bucket containing oats or cubes.

A horsebox or trailer is an essential means of transport if you show your pony. This pony is secured with a quick-release knot.

Tacking up

When tacking up the pony is held or tied up while the saddle is gently put on a little forward of its correct position. It is then slid back into place so that the hairs of the back lie comfortably flat beneath it.

The girth is fastened underneath the pony's belly, but is not tightened at first until the saddle has warmed up and settled on the pony's back.

Next the bridle is put on. The reins are passed over the pony's head so that it can be safely held while the headcollar is removed.

Holding the headpiece in the right hand, the bit is pressed *gently* against the teeth until the pony opens its mouth to accept it.

The headpiece is then lifted over the ears and into place.

Finally the various straps are fastened and checked to see that the bridle fits comfortably, without chafing behind the ears or any other bony areas.

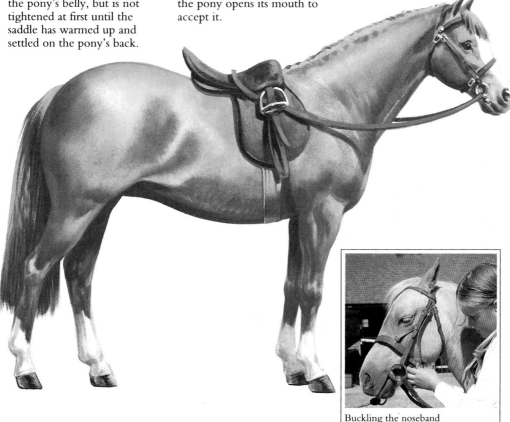

Buckling the noseband

All tack must be kept in perfect condition, being washed and saddle-soaped after each use. Girths and stirrup leathers must be checked for wear. Neglected tack deteriorates very quickly and becomes dangerous in use and expensive to replace.

Exercising

Before buying a pony it is also important to know where you will ride. It may be that riding is not possible at all, unless you are competent to negotiate roads before getting to open country, even if that is within easy reach. Certainly a pony cannot constantly be ridden around its own field or paddock. For one thing it will become decidedly bored; for another, the grass will be seriously damaged. Once the land becomes 'poached', the only way to restore the pasture is to re-seed, and then to allow time for the new grass to mature before letting the pony on it again. In short, it is possible for a pony to destroy the very piece of land that supports it.

The degree of exercise to be given to a pony depends a great deal on its level of fitness. A pony turned out at grass all week and brought in for riding only at weekends will be in soft condition, and must not be raced around or jumped. In order to prepare such a pony for taking part in competitions during school holidays, for example, it must be brought in and its feed and exercise increased until it is fit. At first exercise should be restricted to walking, preferably on roads, for a week or two, then walking may be combined with slow trotting, and then gradually increased periods of schooling can follow the extended road work.

After about six weeks of gradual schooling combined with careful feeding, the pony should be fit enough to tackle most events for which it is suitable. It is slow steady work that conditions a pony, so galloping and even periods of cantering, should be saved until the animal is obviously fit. Always finish the schooling sessions with several minutes of slow, even walking so that the pony cools down and relaxes before returning to its stable. Once the tack is removed, the pony should be checked for any minor injuries such as cuts or bruises, then its feet must be picked out, and the saddle and sweat marks brushed out. When the pony is cool, give him a drink before offering his food.

It is important to note that a pony should not be exercised until at least 1½ hours have elapsed after a heavy feed, or 1 hour after a light feed, or hay.

Lameness is easily detected when riding a pony, and you must immediately dismount. But it is often difficult to detect which leg is affected. If the pony is lame on a foreleg, its head will nod as the sound leg touches the ground. Similarly, when a hind leg is involved the pony's weight will fall on the sound leg. The legs should be felt for signs of heat or swelling, and sometimes a pony will flinch when the painful region is touched. First check the hooves for stones which can cause temporary lameness. *Never* ride a lame pony – lead it home slowly and quietly.

One of the best ways of enjoying the countryside is from horseback. The two riders on the left are making good use of quiet bridleways away from busy traffic, while the keen young rider below takes a safe shortcut by jumping her able pony over a low stone wall.

Basic schooling

A pony should be taught to perform well at all paces and be able to change from the faster to the slower paces without any difficulty. Ponies can become excited in company and run away with their riders, so regular schooling is helpful. Most ponies enjoy being schooled, and if they are in good condition, fit and well-fed, their performance can only be improved by schooling periods.

Schooling consists of carefully formulated and performed series of lessons, with the pony either on the lunging rein, or ridden, or a combination of both. The lessons must never become boring or tiring for the pony and only one major new lesson should be taught in any one session. Once a pony has mastered a new movement, or improved its performance

generally, the schooling session should stop and the pony be praised and retired to digest what has been learned. The following day the new lesson should be tested and reinforced.

It is important to take one small step at a time in schooling and inexperienced riders should attend Pony Club training sessions, or enrol at a local riding school for expert tuition and advice.

The healthy pony

Worms
Ponies should be dosed against intestinal worms at regular intervals. A dung sample should be collected and tested by the vet who will recommend a suitable wormer. Most ponies are easy to dose if the remedial powder is sprinkled into a tasty feed.

Ponies – particularly the native breeds – can be very hardy, yet the horse as a species is not an animal which can withstand disease or injury very well. It is important to maintain constant vigilance and inspect your pony thoroughly at least once a day.

SHOEING

One of the most important routines to establish is that of the care of the pony's feet. Shoeing must be carried out by a qualified farrier or blacksmith on a regular basis, usually every four to six weeks. A pony which does a lot of work on the roads will quickly wear down its shoes. A pony exercised mainly on grass will not wear out its shoes so quickly, but as the hooves grow, the shoes must be taken off, the hooves trimmed, and the shoes refitted. A pony with badly fitted or loose shoes can be dangerous to ride as it could easily come down in a fall that injures itself, and its rider, with serious consequences.

A healthy horse or pony will often enjoy cantering freely around its paddock.

THE VET
The veterinary surgeon can be your pony's best friend. Get to know your local vet specializing in horses when your pony is in good health, by having a routine check-up. In an emergency, the vet will have background knowledge of the animal which may be a help with diagnosis and treatment. Set up a regular health check and vaccination programme for your pony.

VACCINATIONS
Vaccines are available to prevent the pony contracting equine flu, and also against tetanus (see pages 36–37).

SIGNS OF HEALTH
It is only by observing the animal in health that it is possible to learn to recognize problems when they arise. Whenever there is any question about the general health of a pony it is most important to seek veterinary advice without delay rather than try and guess what might be the trouble.

Alertness	judged by a normal response to handling; often a matter of knowing the pony.
Appetite	good; the pony should enjoy its food.
Body condition	well covered, without any obvious signs of obesity. Judgement of condition is a matter of experience.
Coat and skin	free of patchy hair loss, lice, sores and signs of other skin diseases. The appearance of the unclipped coat can vary remarkably with the season – the winter coat can look rough but should be reasonably dense and even. A staring coat that tends to stand open and is of poor texture is often an indication of poor health.
Dung	normally firm and well-formed. It may become less firm at times, for instance when the pony is turned out on to fresh pasture.
Eyes	free from any discharge and showing a healthy pink conjunctiva.
Feet	hooves free from splits or cracks. Shoes should be firmly attached, with no risen clenches.
Gait	normal at all paces, with no sign of lameness.
Nose	free from nasal discharge.
Performance	enthusiastic; the pony should enjoy its exercise. Care must be taken not to confuse loss of fitness with 'laziness'. Apparent laziness usually has a very good reason, ranging from disease to boredom.

Ailments

Seek veterinary advice immediately if you suspect any of the following conditions.

Broken wind Exaggerated breathing noticed when the pony is at rest or only moderately exercised. Associated with permanently damaged lungs, e.g. as a result of being worked with a cough or when unfit.

Colic Abdominal pain due to indigestion, accumulation of gas, or many other reasons. Commonly the result of unsuitable feeding. Always a potentially dangerous condition requiring immediate veterinary advice (see page 38).

Corn An inflamed or bruised area on the sole of the foot, usually towards the heel (at the 'seat of corn'). Lameness may be sudden or progressive. Commonly caused by a stone becoming wedged between shoe and heel, but can be due to poor shoeing or neglect of the overgrown foot.

Cough May result from respiratory infection, but is often caused by dusty hay or bedding. Depending upon the cause, coughs can be highly infectious to other ponies.

Girth gall A progressively sore area of skin (often just behind the elbow) generally due to rubbing or pinching by girths which are poorly maintained.

Influenza (Equine flu) A highly infectious condition due to a virus. Fever, cough, discharge from eyes and nose, together with depression and loss of appetite are all typical symptoms. The condition can be extremely serious and preventative vaccination is recommended.

Lameness Should be investigated as soon as it is detected. If you are riding (this is often the time when lameness is first noticed), dismount immediately and walk the pony home (see page 32). It may be something very minor like a stone in the shoe, but could easily be the start of a much more serious disability. If you are in any doubt, consult a veterinary surgeon.

Laminitis (fever in the feet or 'founder') Typically, this is an extremely painful inflammatory condition involving the sensitive part of the wall of both forefeet. Severely affected animals can hardly move, and may stand like a rocking-horse.

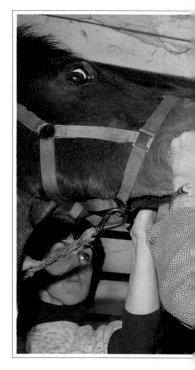

Less severe cases show lameness and a stilted gait. Often seen when ponies are turned out to lush pasture, or as the result of a sudden introduction of certain foods such as clover hay. Laminitis may lead to foot deformities and permanent lameness.

Prick   An injury caused by a nail being driven accidentally into the sensitive part of the wall of the hoof during shoeing. Generally this results in lameness immediately afterwards. A minor form of the same injury is a 'bind'.

Pus in the foot   Usually the result of penetration of the sole by a sharp object, which introduces infection. Lameness (with heat in the foot) can be severe.

Ringworm   A skin disease caused by one of several varieties of fungus. Patchy hair loss, irritation and scab formation are typical signs. The condition is highly contagious and other ponies and humans may also become infected with it.

Saddle sores   The result of local pressure or rubbing from a badly fitting saddle. If neglected, can be serious.

Sore mouth   This generally involves bruising of the delicate tissues around the mouth. Usually the problem is related to 'unsympathetic hands' and a sensitive mouth; or to the use of an unsuitable bit. Occasionally, misshapen or abnormal teeth may cause a sore mouth.

Splint   A bony enlargement, generally on the cannon bone, which forms as the result of repeated stress or an injury. The results vary from a mere blemish to lameness.

Teeth (overgrowth)   See pages 10–11.

Tendon injury   The common injury is a strained tendon as a result of some uncoordinated movement or too heavy a workload in relation to the state of fitness. Such injuries are always potentially serious.

Tetanus   A serious and generally fatal condition involving the nervous system. Tetanus follows infection of a wound by a bacterium commonly found in dung and soil. Vaccination against tetanus is always a wise precaution.

Thrush   An evil-smelling inflammation of the frog of the foot. It is often associated with dirty feet, foul bedding or with poor farriery.

Worms   Most ponies will have some degree of red-worm infestation. To avoid loss of condition, regular worm dosing and proper management of pasture are essential.

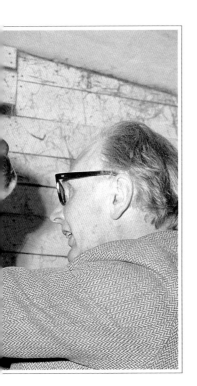

An annual veterinary check-up is advised, including a dental inspection and routine vaccination.

Emergencies

COLIC

A pony showing symptoms of colic will be restless and may sweat and kick up at its stomach. It may also want to roll. If you notice any of these symptoms, contact your vet immediately. While you are waiting for the vet to arrive, keep your pony warm and walk it around. Do not let it roll.

WOUNDS

All wounds should be checked without delay, however trivial they may seem. A puncture caused by a thorn or nail, for example, may appear small but penetration may be deep, with the danger of an abscess forming if the wound is left untreated.

● If the wound is bleeding freely, staunch the flow by applying pressure by bandaging or pressing the heel of the thumb on the wound.

● Clean the wound by flushing with water from a hose-pipe or bathe it with clean cotton wool swabs soaked in saline solution – do not use disinfectant.

● Check that your pony's tetanus vaccinations are up to date.

● Unless the injury is superficial, telephone your vet for advice. And keep your eye on even a small wound in case it does not heal as it should, or begins to suppurate.

First aid kit
A simple first aid kit should be kept in a convenient locked medicine cupboard. All items in the kit should be clearly labelled and used items replaced as soon as possible. Your vet will advise you of what you should keep in stock, but a typical basic kit is illustrated below:

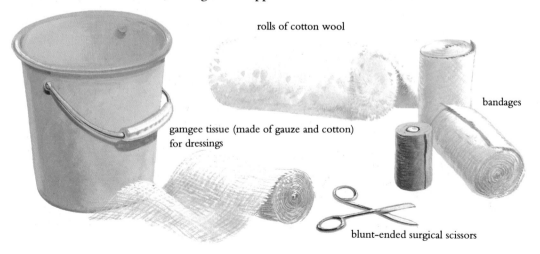

rolls of cotton wool

bandages

gamgee tissue (made of gauze and cotton) for dressings

blunt-ended surgical scissors

Foals

A mare may not be apparently in foal until fairly late in pregnancy, so if you are planning to buy a mare it is advisable to ask the vet to confirm she is not pregnant when the other general health checks are carried out.

Foals are undeniably appealing and it may, to the inexperienced, seem an inexpensive way of acquiring a family pony. However, the rearing of a young pony requires sensitive handling. A foal under the age of six months must never be sold, unless with its dam, and even a hardy breed which will later live out at grass will need stabling at night for the first year.

Serious training will not begin until the foal is three years old, and full work only when it reaches four, but treatment in the formative years is very important in determining how much the foal will benefit from later schooling, and this is best entrusted to experienced hands.

Only breed from a pony if you have the space, time and facilities for the correct care of a foal.

Gymkhanas

Perhaps the most popular sport of all for the pony and its owner is the gymkhana. Every type of pony can have a try at one or other of the many varied events, and great fun is had by all – the riders, the ponies and the spectators. A small nimble pony can often outmanoeuvre a larger one, for many of the games rely on the agility of the pony in cooperation with its rider rather than superior speed or jumping ability.

Some ponies learn to play all the gymkhana games and seem to thoroughly enjoy themselves, turning, stopping and 'riding off' other ponies seemingly without waiting for their rider's signals.

Taking part in gymkhana games develops in a rider an unconscious sense of balance and helps to develop a good, natural seat. In the pony it develops strong hocks and haunches and generally improves agility and handiness.

Gymkhana games are enjoyable for both pony and rider, and improve general agility and obedience.

Lots of careful schooling is necessary for both pony and rider before starting competitive jumping.

In training a pony for gymkhana games and events, basic schooling comes first and the pony is taught to walk, trot and canter, changing pace immediately the aids are applied. The pony must go forward eagerly, and stop promptly from any pace. It must stand still when being mounted, even in the highly charged atmosphere of the crowded ring, and must not be tempted to run when other ponies pass by. It must be taught to accept strange, frightening sights such as the rider frantically attempting to bite an apple from a swinging string, or flapping along half-encased in a bran sack. The pony must learn to run alongside the rider on a loose rein, and be ridden carrying strange objects such as a straw-filled dummy, a bucket, an umbrella or an egg balanced on a long wooden spoon. The pony must learn to go right up to other strange objects to enable the rider to collect or place flags or poles and must often be prepared to race in the opposite direction from all the other ponies in the ring.

The rider, too, needs lots of schooling in order to perform all these exhilarating games without pulling on the pony's mouth, or bringing it down in the excitement.

Pony safety

SECURITY

It is not only valuable racehorses which attract a thief's attention, and a distressing number of family ponies disappear each year. There are several precautions it is sensible to take to reduce the chance of the loss or theft of your pony.

- Keep your pony in at night wherever possible.
- Lock the bottom stable door and consider installing a lockable metal grid in the top door area to allow ventilation but prevent intruders.
- Install security lights to deter intruders from entering stable areas.
- Use padlocks to secure field gates on both sides to prevent them being lifted off their hinges and to prevent unauthorized access by vehicles. Ensure all fences are as secure as possible.
- Leave headcollars off to make it more difficult for a stranger to catch a horse.
- Under the Horsewatch scheme, owners should report *anything* unusual immediately to the police or the local RSPCA.

IDENTIFICATION

Make sure you have a description chart of your horse, and take clear photographs of it from both sides and face on to help with identification. Keep a note of any distinguishing scars or marks. There is no legal requirement to permanently identify or register your pony but the RSPCA strongly recommends that you do. When your pony is registered with a vet you will receive a document which will describe it by its height, colour and markings. However it is better to have your pony permanently identified by an identichip or a freeze mark. More and more ponies are being stolen and permanent identification will offer you the best chance of finding your pony. If your pony is stolen, or if you see a pony that you think may have been stolen, contact your local Horsewatch group. (The British Horse Society will have details, see page 43.)

Safety on the road

DOS

Do read all appropriate sections of the Highway Code, and obtain *Riding and Road Safety*, a booklet from the British Horse Society. Follow the instructions they give at all times.

Do arrange to take the British Horse Society Riding and Road Safety Test – the application form is in the *Riding and Road Safety* booklet.

Do make sure you are fully insured – third party legal liability is important if there is an accident.

Do check your pony's tack and make sure it is correctly fitted before setting off. Also ensure that you are wearing suitable footwear and headgear.

Do make sure you can be seen: fluorescent materials show up well in daylight but have no special qualities when visibility is poor. Tabards of reflective material are very effective, and if you find you have to ride in poor light, you should also fit reflective bands just above your pony's fetlocks.

Do give clear and accurate signals and be considerate of other road users; thank motorists and others who show courtesy – lift a hand in acknowledgement, or smile and nod if you need both hands on the reins.

DON'TS

Do not try to teach a young pony or rider road manners without a steady older pony and experienced rider to help you. A label on a reflective tabard reading 'Young horse' or similar will be a helpful warning to other road users.

Do not ride more than two abreast on the road, or ride too close to walkers or other road users.

Do not ride on roads when there is snow or ice.

Do not panic if your pony slips or starts to fall. Keep calm, hold the front of the saddle and give it a free rein until it finds its feet. If the pony falls and you come off, hold on to the reins, calm the pony and lead it to a quiet place on safe ground before remounting.

Do not attempt to cross a busy road unless you are certain it is safe to do so.

Do not ride at night unless it is unavoidable. When leading a pony in the dark, walk on the left-hand side of the road with the pony on your left. Carry a torch with a white light to the front and a red light showing to the rear. If riding at night, fit a safety lamp to the off-side stirrup, showing white to the front and red to the rear.

British Horse Society, Stoneleigh, Kenilworth, Warwickshire, CV8 2LR. Tel. 0203 696697.

When riding on the road it is vital that you are visible to all other road users.

Your questions answered

How can I work out the cost of keeping a pony?
A little research is a very good idea. Check out the following items; the total should be a reasonably accurate guide to the annual cost of keeping a pony:
- any rent for field/stabling, or livery costs
- 1–2 tonnes of good hay
- pony cubes: about 10–15 large sacks
- worming treatment: 4–6 doses
- tetanus and equine flu injections
- blacksmith: at least 8 visits
- insurance cover

In addition you should allow for miscellaneous expenses such as extra veterinary treatment, repairs and replacements to tack and equipment, extra food in very cold weather, riding lessons and travelling expenses.

How do I insure my pony?
Most major insurance companies insure livestock, and advertise in horse and pony magazines. The premium payable depends on the value of the pony and its lifestyle – competitive ponies, for example, cost more to insure than pet ponies.

To insure your pony you will need a veterinary certificate of health which is often included in the insurance company's proposal form. The insurance policy covers the risk of death by accident, but not from natural causes and you should make sure that the cost of veterinary bills is included, and also insure your tack for loss through theft or damage.

Is there a club or society which will help me take the best possible care of my pony?
Your local branch of the Pony Club, which is the junior branch of the British Horse Society, is well worth joining. You can remain a member until 21 years of age. There is an annual membership fee, plus a small fee payable when you first join. Contact them at: Pony Club Headquarters, The British Equestrian Centre, Stoneleigh, Kenilworth, Warwickshire, CV8 2LR (Tel. 0203 696697).

Does my pony need a New Zealand rug?

Although a New Zealand rug may not be used for much of the year, it is a useful asset if you live in a particularly cold area or there is little adequate shelter in the field. It is indispensable if your pony is old or has been unwell, or if it is obviously cold and miserable. A pony which does strenuous work in winter, and is therefore partially clipped, will also require a New Zealand rug in cold or wet weather. The rug should be taken off and shaken out every day and must not be left on when the pony is brought into a stable, as sweat cannot evaporate through the waterproof layers. For the same reason a New Zealand rug must not be put on a hot, sweating horse which has just been exercising.

How will I know that my pony needs the blacksmith?

You should arrange regular appointments with the blacksmith, but there are specific signs to look out for, which indicate that the pony's feet need attention:
● the ends of the nails which hold the shoe on (clenches) rise above the hoof surface
● the shoe is worn or cracked at the toe
● the shoe twists inwards towards the frog and the horn beings to grow over it
● the hoof grows so long that the frog is no longer in contact with the ground
● the shoe is loose and makes a clinking sound when the pony is ridden, or the shoe comes off altogether.

Are there any special rules for riding in the country?

Ponies can be ridden on all public roads except motorways. They can be ridden on designated bridleways and by-ways, and on common land unless a by-law prevents this, but they must not be ridden on footpaths except with the special permission of the landowner. The Code for Riding Responsibly, which covers courtesy to others and care for the land, should be followed at all times. For a copy of the Code, contact the British Horse Society (see page 43).

I have been told that my pony's haynet might be dangerous. How can it be?

There is nothing dangerous about a haynet itself, but it is important to fix it at just the right height: too high and the dust and scraps of hay it sheds might irritate your pony's eyes and nostrils; too low down and it is easy for your pony to put its hoof through the mesh when the net is empty.

Life history

Scientific name	*Equus caballus*
Name of adult male	entire: stallion castrated: gelding
Name of adult female	mare
Name of young	colt foal (male); filly foal (female)
Gestation period	about 11 months (335 to 350 days); multiple births are extremely rare
Condition at birth	eyes open; able to stand; full coat
Weaning	5 or 6 months minimum
Breeding age	mare: 3 to 20 years (exceptionally) stallions: 2 to 20 years (exceptionally)
Oestrus	every 3 weeks from early spring to midsummer
Retire from work	progressively from about 16 years
Life expectancy	up to 20 years but often longer

Record card

Record sheet for your own pony

photograph or portrait

Name

Date of birth (actual or estimated)

Breed   Sex

Colour/Description   Height

Micro imprint/brand

Feeding notes

Medical record

Vaccination record

Veterinary surgeon's name   Surgery hours

Practice address

                                         Tel. no.

Index